The rising of the Moon

In this series

Art needs no justification: H. R. Rookmaaker
The Bible BC: what can archaeology prove?: A. R. Millard
Christian meditation: Edmund P. Clowney
God incarnate: George L. Carey
Going places: Elizabeth Goldsmith
Guidance: some biblical principles: O. R. Barclay
The homosexual way: a Christian option? David Field
Love is a feeling to be learned: Walter Trobisch
The mark of the Christian: Francis A. Schaeffer
Money matters: Simon Webley
Salt to the world: A. N. Triton
Time with God: Graham Claydon
Your mind matters: John R. W. Stott

The rising of the Moon

An examination of Sun Myung Moon and his Unification Church

John Allan

'I think that, of all God's saints, I am the most successful one.'
                              Sun Myung Moon

Inter-Varsity Press

Inter-Varsity Press
38 De Montfort Street, Leicester LE1 7GP, England

© John Allan 1980

All rights reserved. No part of this publication may be reproduced, stored in a retrieval system, or transmitted, in any form or by any means, electronic, mechanical, photocopying, recording or otherwise, without the prior permission of Inter-Varsity Press.

Unless otherwise stated, quotations from the Bible are from the Revised Standard Version of the Bible, copyrighted 1946, 1952, © 1971, 1973 by the Division of Christian Education of the National Council of the Churches of Christ in the USA, and used by permission.

First published 1980

ISBN 0 85110 236 0

Printed in Great Britain by
Hunt Barnard Printing Ltd.,
Aylesbury, Bucks.

Inter-Varsity Press is the publishing division of the Universities and Colleges Christian Fellowship (formerly the Inter-Varsity Fellowship), a student movement linking Christian Unions in universities and colleges throughout the British Isles, and a member movement of the International Fellowship of Evangelical Students. For information about local and national activities in Great Britain write to UCCF, 38 De Montfort Street, Leicester LE1 7GP.

Preface

Thanks are due to all sorts of people for the final shape of this book: to David Johnson, vicar of Stratton St Margaret, for his unfailing help and generous provision of research material; to Philip Hand, Caryl Williams and Deo Gloria Trust for many incidental kindnesses; and to my wife Anthea, for putting up cheerfully with nocturnal typewriting noises and Unification documents all over the carpet. This book is dedicated, first, to James Bjornstadt, with enormous respect and admiration; and, secondly, to Luigi, George, Edward and Nick, members of the Unification Church. May they read it with an open mind.

Contents

Preface	5
1 Moonrise	7
2 The hidden message of the Bible	10
3 The Lord of the Second Advent	16
4 'God's interpretation'?	20
5 Beneath the surface	34
6 'I am your brain'	51
7 For Christians only	58
Additional note: Other names used by the Unification Church in Britain	61
Valuable books for further reading	62

1
Moonrise

'I felt elated,' said Henry Masters. 'To suddenly find something you feel you've been looking for all your life.'[1] Masters, the squire of the Wiltshire village of Stanton Fitzwarren, had just handed over £800,000-worth of property – which had been in his family for 400 years – to a smiling Korean millionaire.

Post Offices, confectionery works and fishing boats . . . the list of valuable goods that have been given away to Sun Myung Moon is a strange one. The followers of this self-styled prophet range from Portuguese labourers to the heir to a biscuit empire; but to a man they assert that they have found in following Moon's teaching a satisfaction and peace that no amount of money could have have brought them. Considering that Moon was virtually unknown in the West before 1972 – and considering that he is now personally worth £8 million – what is the secret of his success? What can account for 'the rising of the Moon'?

Sun Myung Moon was born in a Korean farming village on 6 January, 1920, the second of eight children of a Presbyterian farmer. Early in his life, he came under the influence of an odd type of messianic pentecostal group, who encouraged visions and emphasized the importance of dreams; this led to his now-famous mountainside vision, when at the age of sixteen (he claims) he saw Christ appear to him. Christ 'revealed that he was destined to accomplish a great mission in which Jesus would work with him'.[2] This was just the prelude to a series of visions and revelations in which Jesus gradually became more familiar and explicit about the nature of the job; he

[1] *New Tomorrow* 5 (Dec. 1977), p. 26.
[2] Young Oon Kim, *The Divine Principle and its Application* (New York, n.d.), p. vii.

'embraced him as a brother and asked him to complete his desire to build the Kingdom of Heaven on earth'.[3]

In 1945 came the most important experience. His Church is not so keen to disclose details of this vision as of the 1936 one, but the later experience was the real foundation of Moon's ministry. In it, we are told, Jesus bowed down to him and hailed him as master; Moon had now surpassed Jesus in dignity.

> At that moment, he became the absolute victor of heaven and earth. The whole spirit world bowed down to him on that day of victory . . . The spirit world has already recognized him as the victor of the universe and the Lord of creation.[4]

It was, however, another nine years before the Tong-il Kyo, or Holy Spirit Association for the Unification of World Christianity, emerged in the form we know today. The Church was founded in association with Yee Hye Wen, a former medical student with an amazingly brilliant mind. So badly crippled was Yee that he could not sit, but he made up for his physical disability with feats of mental agility. Together with Moon he codified and regularized the 'Principles' which the 'Messiah' had assimilated. Yee also invented the revolutionary airgun which would eventually be the cornerstone of Moon's commercial empire.

Fiercely anti-Communist, skilfully blending the orthodoxy of Bible quotations with the exotic allure of spirit experiences, Moon's brand of Korean nationalist Christianity soon attracted a wide following. And it spread outside Korea; as early as January 1959, one of his followers had arrived as a student in the USA. But thirteen more years passed before January 1972, when God is said to have given Moon the message which was to make him

[3] *New Tomorrow* 5 (Dec. 1977), p. 25.
[4] *Sun Myung Moon: A Biography* (New York, n.d.), p. 6.

an international celebrity: 'Go to America.'

Before Moon's arrival, the Western world's experience of the Unification Church had been neither impressive nor inspiring. For one thing, according to Moon's calculations, the world had been due for transforming and perfecting by 1967, and it had been imperative that 144,000 converts should be mustered by that year. It failed to happen; and, not surprisingly, the time-scheme has been readjusted and left less definite. 1967, we are told, was only the end of the first of three seven-year periods which will lead to perfection. And the length of the final period could vary quite a bit; 'seven' is just a symbolic number.

Moon arrived as a 'permanent resident alien' in 1973, and immediately set about making a large-scale impact on American society. Within five years, he was claiming 30,000 members in the USA, 6,000 in West Germany, 3,000 in Great Britain, 2,000 in Holland and 1,000 in France. 300,000 people are said to have attended his Washington Monument Rally in 1976. (Actually, these figures are gross over-estimates; likelier figures are 10,000 members in the USA, 500 in Britain, and a 50,000 crowd at the Washington Monument. But then even 50,000 people seems a sizeable audience for a preacher who knew no English and spoke in Korean.)

What has been the secret of this amazing growth, which has won Moon audiences with Eisenhower, Nixon and other world leaders, but which has also provoked the hostility of the world's press and parents' organizations? What sort of theological notions provide the fuel for this powerful lift-off? These are the questions to which I now want to turn.

2
The hidden message of the Bible

So much has been said about the 'brainwashing' activities of the Unification Church that many Christians have a very contemptuous attitude to its beliefs. The general attitude seems to be 'If they can't convince people they're right without mental pressure, their theories must be pretty flimsy.' But in fact Sun Myung Moon can make out a subtler case for his beliefs than many Christians would think; and everything is backed with biblical evidence. In this chapter and the next, I want to outline the Unification theory without comment, and reserve judgment until chapter 4.

After all, says Moon, 'There is only one God, one Christ, one Bible. Today, however, in the Christian world alone there are more than 400 different denominations, all looking at the Bible from very different points of view, with many different interpretations.'[1] But if we could get away from *man's* theories about the Bible, and discover *God's* interpretation – ah, then we could unify world Christianity.

People disagree about the Bible's message because it is written in symbols and parables, which must be deciphered correctly. Take the story of the fall, for instance. Can we really believe that absurd story about eating a fruit? Surely not; doesn't Matthew 15:11 say that nothing edible can cause a man to fall? If so, the 'fruit' in the story must be a symbol for something else – something stimulating, and ardently desired.

Furthermore, the trees in the story are just symbols too. The 'tree of life' wasn't an actual tree; this phrase is used throughout the Bible (Proverbs 12:12; Revelation 22:14) to signify the *state of perfected manhood*. Thus the 'tree of life' represents Adam, or rather what Adam would

[1] *The New Future of Christianity* (London, 1974), p. 69.

have become, if only he had obeyed God. What about the other tree, the 'tree of the knowledge of good and evil'? Well, logically it represents perfected *womanhood*, Eve.

What, then, can the fruit be? We gain a clue from Jude 6 and 7. This passage identifies the original sin of the angels with the sin of Sodom and Gomorrah. As everyone knows, these towns were famous for one thing only – illicit sex. Thus the original sin of the angel Lucifer must have been sex with Eve.

After sharing her 'fruit' with the serpent, Eve shared some with her husband. In other words, she slept with him too, in order to restore her lost innocence. Alas, instead she passed on the corruption to Adam as well, and he fell from grace.

We can see that this interpretation is correct when we look at what they did next. Significantly, they covered the lower half of their bodies.

> If they had committed sin by eating an actual fruit of a 'tree of the knowledge of good and evil', they would have concealed their hands and mouths instead. It is the nature of man to conceal an area of transgression. They covered their sexual parts, clearly indicating that they were ashamed of the sexual areas of their bodies because they had sinned through them.[2]

Eve's intercourse with Lucifer means that the first human baby – Cain – was fathered by Satan.[3] And this is why Jesus says in John 8:44 that human beings are 'of your father the devil'.

In our veins the blood of fornication is running; the blood of murder is running through our veins; we are

[2] *Divine Principle* (Thornton Heath, 1973), p. 72.

[3] It is only fair to state that this conclusion – inescapably as it seems to follow from Moon doctrine as I have read it – was specifically denied by Mike Marshall, Public Affairs Director of the Unification Church in Great Britain, when we met in a public meeting.

in the blood lineage of murderers . . . Terrible blood is running in our veins.[4]

Thus the purpose of God's creation has been frustrated, and his world has turned into a sick, nightmare caricature of what he intended. Let's stop for a moment and look at what God *did* intend. In creation, everything exists in dual relationships – male and female, subject and object, outward form and inward essence. God is like that too (he must be, for he created us 'in his own image'). The law of creation is that every *subject* must have an *object* to relate to; and God created the world to play 'object' to his 'subject'. The whole creation 'is His body or outward form'.[5] 'He makes His presence known in the totality of creation which serves as His body . . . providing the outer form of His being.'[6]

God projected Adam and Eve out of himself, 'external and objective manifestations of the polarity of God'.[7] Their first task was to pass through the stages of Formation, Growth and Perfection, and reach complete maturity. Tragically, they hadn't yet reached this last stage when Lucifer made his seduction bid.

Thus human history consists of a catalogue of God's attempts to undo the evil of the fall and restore mankind. But this hasn't happened yet. Why? Isn't God supposed to be all-powerful? It must be because 'in order to fulfil the purpose of creation, man's effort is as absolutely essential as God's'.[8] Unless we accomplish *our* 'portion of responsibility' God's plan breaks down, and he has to wait for another generation to arrive before he tries again.

Actually, the fall could have been sorted out very

[4] *120 Day Training Program* (New York, n.d.), p. 80.

[5] Young Oon Kim, *The Divine Principle and its Application*, p. 2.

[6] Young Oon Kim, *Unification Theology and Christian Thought* (New York, 1975), p. 7.

[7] Young Oon Kim, *The Divine Principle and Its Application*, pp. 3, 11.

[8] Statement made on side one of cassette tape entitled *Divine Principle Lecture*, issued by the Unification Church in London.

quickly – if only Cain had humbled himself before Abel and obeyed him. Cain represented Satan, Abel God, and bowing to Abel would have restored a proper balance. Instead, Abel was killed.

God's next attempt was Noah, but that failed too – because Noah got drunk and cavorted around with no clothes on. Not that this was the disqualifying sin! Noah was quite right to become intoxicated, because it recreated in his heart the sort of joyful feeling Adam could have had in the garden if he had not sinned. And in his joy Noah was unashamed of his nakedness, because alcohol had helped him to forget the guilt of the original sexual sin.

No, continues Moon, the failure here was Ham, Noah's eldest son. Instead of understanding and rejoicing with his father, he tried to cover him up, thus restoring the guilt of the fall. God sighed, and prepared to wait another 1,600 years for the next attempt.

Abraham was the next failure: not for allowing his wife to be possessed by another man; not for turning his slave-girl and illegitimate son out to die; but for neglecting to cut some birds in half during a sacrifice in Genesis 15. And so the failures continue: Moses struck the rock twice . . . Solomon went after foreign women . . . Jesus . . .

What of Jesus? The Unification Church hotly deny that Jesus 'failed' in his mission. He did all that he could. But, they argue, he was let down badly by those who should have believed in him.

Jesus was a man, like any other, with one crucial difference: he was sinless. He had fulfilled the purpose of creation. And this means that he 'is one body with God. So, in light of his deity, he may well be called God. Nevertheless, he can by no means be God himself.'[9] Jesus is no more God than Adam could have been – or anyone else who manages to fulfil creation's purpose.

And although he was special, Jesus' birth was quite

[9] *Divine Principle*, pp. 210–211.

mundane. Far from being the son of a virgin, he was illegitimately born to Zechariah the priest, who had an affair with Mary. This meant that he combined in himself the priestly lineage (through Zechariah) and the kingly lineage of David (through Mary) and was thus equipped to be ideal king. It also made him half-brother to John the Baptist.

Now *this* strange figure, says Moon, is the real reason for Jesus' failure.

> Today, it is very shocking when we understand that the people of Israel couldn't believe Jesus. But it is also shocking and really unbelievable that John the Baptist, God's elected prophet, who was sent specifically to straighten the way of the Lord, denied Him. If John the Baptist had not only accepted and witnessed to Jesus Christ as the son of God, but had followed him, becoming his disciple, then their destinies would have coincided.[10]

John must have impressed the Jews very deeply. Son of a distinguished priestly family, with miracles surrounding his birth, he lived an exemplary life of self-discipline in the wilderness. The Jews would have trusted his word far sooner than that of Jesus.

Jesus said that John was really Elijah come back (Matthew 17:10ff). But when the Pharisees asked John, 'Are you Elijah?' he denied it,[11] thus making Jesus out to be a liar. And then in Matthew 11 John even sent his disciples to ask Jesus if he really *was* the Messiah, 'or should we wait for another?' Indignant at this faithlessness, Jesus refused to answer yes or no. He merely replied, 'Blessed is he who takes no offence at me,' an implied rebuke. Then

---

[10] Sun Myung Moon, 'Christmas in Heart', *New Tomorrow* 5 (Dec. 1977), p. 23.
[11] John 1:21.

he added that John would be 'least in the kingdom of heaven' because of his lack of faith.

With John's support, Jesus could have ruled the nation. He could have married and founded a perfect family, to restore the purpose of creation. But in these circumstances he couldn't, and his life was full of grief.

> I challenge anyone to deny that when we see the life of Jesus we see nothing but sorrow and pain . . . we see a life . . . of constant sorrow right to the very moment of death.[12]

> Although Jesus came as the Messiah, Jesus couldn't be the Messiah . . . poor, poor Jesus. He couldn't be Messiah on earth.[13]

Christians usually think that when Jesus remarked, 'The poor have good news preached to them' (Matthew 11:5), he was quite glad about it. Not so, argues *Divine Principle*. Jesus was very sad that because of John's defection he had only a bunch of fishermen, harlots and tax collectors for an audience. He was never going to be accepted by the people who really mattered in society; and so he realized that he could fulfil only half of his life's mission. He would have to die.

Jesus' crucifixion was never part of God's plan. It was only 'God's painful alternative'. When Jesus said, 'It is finished,' he 'did not mean by that he had accomplished the entire scope of his mission. He merely meant that his life and work were over.'[14] As Jesus died, God gave his body to Satan as a ransom for the souls of men, and Satan invaded Jesus' body. Because of this, men's *souls* can be set free from sin, *but not their bodies*.

---

[12] Ruth Ann Emerson, 'The Broken Heart of God', *New Tomorrow* 4 (Nov. 1977), p. 29.
[13] *120 Day Training Program*, p. 286.
[14] *Divine Principle*, pp. 151–152.

If Jesus had lived, so the teaching goes, he could have restored perfect sinlessness to men. As it is, even the greatest Christians cannot avoid sinning sometimes. This is because Jesus achieved only 'spiritual salvation' for us. 'Physical salvation' is still to come.

Who can bring it?

Answer: the Lord of the Second Advent.

3
The Lord of the Second Advent

Throughout history, argues Sun Myung Moon, God has had a habit of succeeding at the third attempt. He failed with Adam. He failed with Jesus. Now, the time is right for a third Adam, the 'Lord of the Second Advent', to appear and complete the job of salvation.

When is he due to appear?

Divine Principle points out that the history of Christianity so far runs exactly parallel to the history of Israel. Israel spent 400 years in Egypt; and the church was persecuted by the Roman Empire for 400 years. Israel was ruled by judges for 400 years; which corresponds exactly to the 400 years of the Church Fathers. Then there were a united Israelite kingdom (120 years) and a divided one (400 years); while in church history a united Christian empire (120 years) was followed by four centuries of the Eastern and the Western empire. The seventy years of Hebrew exile match the seventy years of the exile of the papacy, and the 140-year Israelite return matches the 140 years of the Renaissance, ending in 1517. The next event for Israel was a 400-year wait for Jesus' coming.

This, of course, indicates that the Lord of the Second Advent will appear 400 years after 1517. About the end of the First World War. Not a great distance, in fact, from 6 January 1920...

Where will the Lord of the Second Advent come from? Not Israel this time; for Jesus announced to the Jews quite clearly, 'I tell you, the kingdom of God will be taken away from you and given to a nation producing the fruits of it' (Matthew 21:43). Which nation would God choose?

Revelation 7:2 is the crucial clue. In that verse, the angel who will arise 'from the rising of the sun' is Lord of the Second Advent. 'The rising of the sun' indicates that he will be born in an Eastern nation – Korea, Japan or China. China is ruled out straight away because her Communism is the ultimate fruit of the way of Cain; Japan was a totalitarian nation in the Second World War, and persecuted the Christians of Korea. Thus there is only one nation in which Messiah could possibly be born. This time, he must be a Korean.

'But', someone will object, 'why do we need another Messiah? Isn't Christ coming back?'

Indeed he is, answers the Unification Church. But must he bear the same identity? After all, Malachi promised that Elijah would return (Malachi 4:5) – and he turned out to be John the Baptist. Why shouldn't Jesus turn out to be someone else?

Again, Daniel promised (Daniel 7:13) that the son of man would come 'with the clouds of heaven' – but instead Jesus was born as a baby in a stable. Perhaps Christians are wrong to expect Jesus to return visibly and powerfully. After all, he is to come 'like a thief in the night' – and thieves are not noted for advertising their arrival.

At first sight, Revelation 1:7 seems to upset this theory.

Behold, he is coming with the clouds, and every eye

will see him, every one who pierced him; and all tribes of earth will wail on account of him.

This verse says that everyone will see Jesus return. But Jesus is in a spiritual body now, which is invisible to unbelievers (Acts 7:55). So if he were to return in spirit form, not everyone could see him. No, he must be returning in a solid human body. And if so, 'the Lord, in the flesh, cannot come on the clouds, so the 'clouds' are surely symbolic'.[1]

What, then, do the clouds signify? Clouds are nothing but vapourized, purified water. And in Revelation 17:15, says Moon, 'water' symbolizes fallen men.

Then we may understand that the clouds would signify the devout saints, whose minds are always in heaven and not on earth, completely reborn from the fallen race of men.[2]

And so the Lord will arrive unseen by the world, but greeted by devout saints who will follow him, in the land of Korea around 1920. This makes it obvious who the Unification Church really believes its leader to be. Official statements are always evasive; but the hymns the 'family' sing to him show clearly his supposed status – Lord of Creation, Master of Jesus, True Parent of Mankind.

Korea, heart of the earth,
You were chosen to give him birth,
Land of the morning calm;
From your hidden springs
Comes a healing balm for all men.

He has come!
His face is like the sun and the moon.

[1] *Ibid.*, p. 513.
[2] *Ibid.*, p. 514.

And soon the world will know his light;
There will be no more night.[3]

Devotees are told amazing stories about Father Moon's supernatural rank and powers.

> One day we asked Father, 'How can you understand what is happening all over the world?' . . . Father said he can give directions to the angels and the angels will go at once. They can bring everything to Father. It is better than the telephone.[4]

> The other day Father came and said that when he was in prison God came and slept with him and embraced him.[5]

> He is greater than the universe. He's more precious than the universe. It is only he from whom sinless mankind can start. He is the only man in the universe by loving whom my sin is solved, by loving whom I can be born anew, by loving whom I can be given rebirth and new life.[6]

To love Father is obviously very important. Church members are encouraged to use pictures of Moon, to 'feel as if'[7] Moon is physically present with them all day long. ('The first idea we have in the morning must be "how about Father". The last idea we have before we go to sleep should be "how about Father".')[8] Sara Pierron recalled for other Moonies her experiences during training:

> When Father trained us, Father said at one point that the sisters could fall in love with Father and think of him in a romantic way as well as our Father and that

[3] The 'Blessing Song'.
[4] *120 Day Training Program*, p. 196.
[5] *Ibid.*, p. 185. [6] *Ibid.*, p. 155. [7] *Ibid.*, p. 157. [8] *Ibid.*, p. 150.

the brothers should think of Mother [Moon's wife] in a romantic way. He said we could feel a closer bond through that and could somehow live in an intoxicated state thinking about our True Parents.[9]

Small wonder that when one girl left the Church 'for about a month . . . I still couldn't look at a picture of Moon. I just couldn't stand to look at him, because I had loved him so much.'[10]

But does Sun Myung Moon merit all the affection he demands? 'No one can come to my depth of relationship with God,' he claims. 'God is crazy for Father.'[11] Simple truth – or breathtaking arrogance? Let us examine the biblical evidence.

4
'God's interpretation'?

The Rev. Thomas Boslooper was a Dutch Reformed minister for nearly thirty years before he met the Moonies. The encounter changed his life. 'The thought occurred to me,' he said, 'over the period of a year, that the formation and development of Unification Theology . . . signals the most radical, powerful and constructive force for the future of Biblical studies since the Protestant Reformation.'[1]

[9] *Ibid.*, p. 345.
[10] Ronald Enroth, *Youth, Brainwashing and the Extremist Cults* (Exeter, 1977), p. 121.
[11] *120 Day Training Program*, p. 118.
[1] T. Boslooper, 'The Religious Nature and Theology of the Unification Church', *The Unification Church: A Documentary Supplement* (Reading, 1977), p. 3.

Impressive words, from a trained theologian; though it must be borne in mind that he is now employed by Moon, and left his own church because of his Unification views. But he insists, 'The truth is that the Unification movement is very authentically Christian.'[2] Is this so? Has *Divine Principle* really captured 'God's interpretation' of the Bible?

If it has, it would appear that God holds a low opinion of his own book. 'We must realize,' proclaims *Divine Principle*, 'that Biblical words are a means of expressing the truth and are not the truth itself . . . the New Testament was given as a textbook for the teaching of truth to the people of 2,000 years ago, people whose spiritual and intellectual standard was very low, compared to that of today.'[3] We might question whether our strife-torn, materialistic century really has a higher 'spiritual standdard' than the first century AD; but let it pass 'Today the truth must appear with a higher standard and with a scientific method of expression in order to enable intelligent modern man to understand it.'[4]

Unlikely as it may seem, the superseding of the New Testament was the real meaning of Joseph's dream in Genesis 37. Joseph dreamt that the sun, moon and stars bowed to him. Sun Myung Moon, the first man in history to understand the dream correctly, explains that this means that the sun and moon (Jesus and the Holy Spirit) accompanied by the stars (the saints of God) would submit to the Lord of the second Advent and acknowledge his authority.

The Holy Spirit, incidentally, is female (which raises the intriguing question why 'she' is referred to consistently by Jesus as 'he'), and has been until now one of the True Parents of humanity – the other being Jesus. Times, however, have changed; Matthew 24:29 predicts that before

[2] *Ibid.*, p. 3.
[3] *Divine Principle*, p. 131.
[4] *Ibid.*, p. 131.

the Lord of the Second Advent arrives, the sun will be darkened, the moon withhold its light, and the stars fall from heaven.

This means that Jesus and the Holy Spirit will be superseded, the New Testament will 'lose its light', and many saints 'will offend the Lord and fail'[5] By contrast, Moon and his wife will become True Parents instead, and his words *(Divine Principle)* the new Bible.

Thus, conveniently, the Unification Church can plunder the Bible for proof-texts for their doctrines, but need not worry too much about bits that don't seem to fit. 'Until our mission with the Christian church is over,' comments Moon, in a secret internal document, 'we must quote the Bible . . . After we receive the inheritance of the Christian, we will be free to teach without the Bible.'[6] He sounds keen to reach that day.

And so Moon can adopt a fairly cavalier attitude to the actual New Testament text. If the Gospel of Matthew slightly contradicts his ideas, it can be blamed on Matthew's 'slanted viewpoint' and false philosophy of history. If the Gospel of John doesn't quite fit, it is because 'the author wanted to reinterpret the life and death of Jesus in the light of his own belief.'[7]

There seems to be something circular about an argument which begins by relying upon an out-of-context exposition of a few words in Matthew, and then proceeds to comment that Matthew is intrinsically untrustworthy anyway. And Moon never explains why the information of explosive importance – that Jesus' words would someday 'lose their light' – was concealed in the most inscrutable, impenetrable symbols, while claims like these stand out stark and clear:

All scripture is inspired by God and profitable for

[5] *Ibid.*, p. 118.
[6] *Master Speaks* (Mar./Apr. 1965), p. 1.
[7] *The Mission of Jesus* (Reading, n.d.), p. 46.

teaching, for reproof, for correction, and for training in righteousness, that the man of God may be complete, equipped for every good work.[8]

(Jesus said) Heaven and earth will pass away, but my words will not pass away.[9]

It looks almost as if God wanted to give us the wrong impression.

Even *Divine Principle*, however, is incomplete; the *120 Day Training Program* mentions casually that Father Moon has yet to reveal two-thirds of his message. In the meantime we can check the reliability of his words by having a spirit revelation.

If you pray deeply, sometimes Heavenly Father can teach you directly. Try to find desperately, and pray desperately, and maybe in the early morning, just before getting up, when you are in the transitional period between sleeping and waking, you might be given a revelation or inspiration. Sometimes a very, very clear answer will be given.[10]

Divine Principle appeals repeatedly to the spirit world for verification. (For instance, 'any Christian who, in spiritual communication, can see John the Baptist directly in the spirit world will be able to understand the authenticity of all these things').[11] Interestingly, few mediums and spiritualist teachers have expressed any respect for Moon at all. Obviously they are getting a very different message from the spirits!

Who is right? Or are they both being fooled? For, it seems, Moonies sometimes receive dubious, untrustworthy messages:

[8] 2 Timothy 3:16.
[9] Mark 13:31.
[10] *120 Day Training Program*, p. 16.
[11] *Divine Principle*, p. 163.

> Don't obey spiritual world but obey Father. Whatever the spiritual world might say about your own blessing, don't believe that but just obey Father.[12]

Amazingly, Ken Sudo then goes on to undermine the whole basis of 'spirit' evidence – and so contradicts the sacred *Divine Principle* – by saying:

> Even the spiritual world is a fallen world, therefore you cannot rely on spiritual world. So don't think a revelation is excellent because it came from spiritual world.[13]

'Do not believe every spirit,' comments the Bible tersely, 'but test the spirits to see whether they are of God.' And the test? 'Every spirit which does not confess Jesus is not of God.'[14] If this is the case, then the spirit guides of the Unification Church seem to be of extremely questionable origin.

It would be impossible to answer briefly all of the theological points raised in our last two chapters. But I would like now to examine one or two of the most important.

The fall

Nothing in Moon's theology contradicts the Bible more blatantly than his ideas about the first human sin. The whole argument is based on a series of flimsy premises which simply fall apart when steadily examined.

For example, look at his reading of the 'symbols'. If the tree of life really means 'perfect manhood', one would like more proof than a couple of isolated verses from such remote contexts as Proverbs and Revelation. But there *is* no more proof. Moreover, even if the tree did mean 'perfected manhood', what this implies is '*person*hood' – not 'masculinity'. The Bible nowhere suggests any dis-

[12] *120 Day Training Program*, p. 142.
[13] *Ibid.*, p. 141.
[14] 1 John 4:1–3.

tinctively *male* characteristics about the tree of life. Thus it does not at all follow that the other tree has to be female, connected with Eve.

Furthermore, if 'eating the fruit of the tree' meant copulation with Lucifer, one would expect *Lucifer* to eat the fruit – not Eve. The symbolism doesn't add up. The fruit is supposed to be 'the symbol of Eve's love'; so what was Eve doing, consuming her own fruit? If anything, it suggests that the serpent tempted her to masturbation, not intercourse.

Of course, the proof-text for Lucifer's sexual involvement is the Jude reference to Sodom and Gomorrah (verses 6–7). Leaving aside the unlikelihood of having to turn to the second-to-last book of the Bible to explain the first story in it, we should notice three things about these verses: first, they are talking about *angels* (plural) who are permanently fettered, without Satan's freedom of movement (Job 1:7), and so may not refer to Lucifer at all; secondly, it is the *punishments*, not the *crimes*, that are spoken of as identical; and thirdly, they list two crimes of Sodom – not one. 'Immoral acts' could admittedly describe intercourse with Eve; but 'unnatural lust'? This is the Bible's phrase for homosexual activity. On the evidence of this, it would seem more logical to believe that Lucifer – not Eve – was the one who slept with Adam.

Didn't Jesus say that 'nothing edible' could defile a man? As ever, Moon has taken a verse right out of its context. In this passage, Jesus is saying that specific acts do not determine sin; it's the inward attitude of heart that counts. It was not the *fruit* that defiled Eve; there was nothing magic about it. Her 'defilement' was caused by her inner attitude of rebellion and defiance.

And finally, is it really natural for a person to 'cover the area of transgression' when he has done something wrong? If we kick out at someone in a fit of temper, do we try to conceal our feet afterwards? If we eavesdrop on someone, do we cover up our ears? The claim is ridiculous.

But it demonstrates the desperation of *Divine Principle* to shore up the collapsing walls of its indefensible account with any argument that will serve.

God

One of the few things on which Christians of different schools have always agreed has been the nature of God. Augustine summed up the general view:

> For Thou didst create heaven and earth, not of Thyself, for then they would be equal . . . even to Thee . . . Therefore, out of nothing didst Thou create heaven and earth.[15]

No orthodox Christian has ever advanced the idea that God created the world out of himself. Yet Moon has. Christians have always stressed the discontinuity between God and his creation, that the one cannot become the other; yet *Divine Principle* claims that people can become God.

This happens when a man becomes perfect. God intends us to be perfect, says Moon; look at Matthew 5:48 – 'You, therefore, must be perfect, even as your heavenly Father is perfect.'

'Perfect' here, however, doesn't mean 'sinless'. This Greek word, *teleios*, is best translated 'mature', 'complete', 'adult'. It is *never* used to refer to a state of being unable to do anything wrong. Paul (Moon's favourite example of a sinful Christian!) applies it to himself in Philippians 3:15.[16]

'In a way,' claims Father Moon, 'God fears man.'[17] This is because God cannot foretell exactly which way

---

[15] Augustine, *Confessions* 13:7.

[16] Paul himself never claimed sinlessness, even towards the end of his life; *cf.* 1 Timothy 1:15.

[17] Sun Myung Moon, 'The Future of Christianity, Part II', *New Tomorrow* 8 (Mar. 1978), p. 22.

man will choose to go. (But what about 1 Peter 1:2 and the whole doctrine of the foreknowledge of God?) This is why God had to give 'contradictory' prophecies in the Old Testament – some saying that Jesus would succeed, some that he would be crucified. Thus, whatever happened, God would be 50% correct.

This poor, weak, bewildered deity is nothing like the God of the Bible. 'The promise of the Lord proves true,' insists Psalm 18:30. 'My word . . . shall not return to me empty,' declares God, 'but it shall accomplish that which I purpose.'[18] Hardly the broken-hearted, powerless pensioner envisaged by the *Training Program*:

> Can you imagine the real situation of Heavenly Father? He was old, 6,000 years old or more. Old man. Shedding blood and shouting He couldn't do anything. Just imagine this is your father. Who made him so miserable? It's me.[19]

There are many more inconsistencies. The Bible insists that new life in Jesus is a free gift from God (Romans 6:23); the *Program* claims that it is impossible for God to give anything unconditionally. In Moon's movement, the merits of your ancestors can win you favour with God and a head start in life; in the Bible, God 'shows no partiality'.[20] Jesus was convinced that his 'sheep' could never be plucked from their security in his hand;[21] *Divine Principle* talks about 'saints' who have 'manifested devout faith' yet become proud and lose 'in an instant the merit they gained through long and bitter trials';[22] all because of a gift which God unwisely gave them:

[18] Isaiah 55:11.
[19] *120 Day Training Program*, p. 231.
[20] Romans 2:11, 1 Peter 1:17.
[21] John 10:28.
[22] *Divine Principle*, p. 179.

> Those with powers of spiritual communication are liable to become antichrists; upon receiving the revelation that they are lords they may act wrongly . . . This is actually why it was prophesied that in the Last Days there would appear many antichrists.[23]

Can Christians become 'antichrists'? The apostle John had a different idea. 'They went out from us,' he said, *'but they were not of us*: for if they had been of us, they would have continued with us.' Significantly for Sun Myung Moon, he then adds:

> This is the antichrist, he who denies the Father and the Son. No-one who denies the Son has the Father.[24]

If we now look at what Sun Myung Moon has to say about the Son – Jesus Christ – it will not take long to see what John would have thought him to be.

Jesus

Ask any Moonie on the street, 'Do you believe that Jesus Christ is God?' and – assuming he has identified you as a Christian – he will answer, 'Yes'. But the truth is not so simple, as a glance at *Divine Principle* reveals.

> Jesus, being one body with God, may be called a second God (image of God), but he can by no means be God Himself.[25]

In other words, Jesus both is God, and isn't. This double-think runs right through the Moon presentation of Jesus. There is an amazing paragraph in *Divine Principle* which begins with the proposition, 'Jesus may well be called the Creator,' then dives into a maze of Unification jargon

[23] *Ibid.*, p. 178.
[24] 1 John 2:18–23.
[25] *Divine Principle*, p. 211.

('substantial encapsulation', 'portion of responsibility', 'perfected individuality'), and finally emerges again with its conclusion, a completely contrasting statement: 'The Bible ... does not signify that he, Jesus, was the Creator Himself.'[26]

Was Jesus God, or not? Was he simply a convenient created being, or was he actually there with God the Father before creation began? Jesus personally had no doubt ('Father, glorify thou me in thy own presence with the glory which I had with thee before the world was made'),[27] and nor had his earliest followers:

> He is the image of the invisible God, the first-born of all creation; for in him all things were created, in heaven and on earth, visible and invisible, whether thrones or dominions or principalities or authorities – all things were created through him and for him. He is before all things, and in him all things hold together.[28]

Nobody before Sun Myung Moon has ever voiced the startling theory that Jesus was the son of Zechariah. Considering the priest's advanced age, and his lack of success in fathering children until that point, it would appear unlikely that he should impregnate two women (in complete defiance, too, of his priestly vows) within six months. Needless to say, there is not a scrap of evidence for the Zechariah theory, while the idea of the virgin birth is supported both by New Testament evidence and by historical traditions that go right back to the beginning of Christianity.

As for the end of his life, the Unification theory that he rose again only as 'a spirit man of the divine stage'[29] flies completely in the face of Scripture. Jesus rose physically;

---

[26] *Ibid.*, p. 211.
[27] John 17:5.
[28] Colossians 1:15–17.
[29] *Divine Principle*, p. 360.

this is the clear teaching of the entire New Testament. The risen Jesus even invited his disciples to 'handle me and see, for a spirit has not flesh and bones as you see that I have'.[30]

Did Jesus' mission fail? Was the crucifixion no part of God's plan? Strange, then, that Jesus testified to having 'accomplished the work which thou gavest me to do';[31] that the crucifixion is claimed to be 'according to the *definite plan* and foreknowledge of God';[32] that Hebrews 10:14 sees no difference between 'spiritual' and 'physical' salvation: 'By a single offering he has perfected for all time those who are sanctified.' There is simply no way of squaring the Bible's claims about Jesus with those of *Divine Principle*. Ultimately, one has to choose between the two. And if the Bible is right? Then he who denies the Son, has not the Father either . . .

The Lord of the Second Advent

Moon's whole theory about himself depends desperately upon the accuracy of his mathematical calculations. If his figures are wrong, and Messiah is due to be born in, say, 1990, his credibility vanishes straight away. How accurate are they?

The answer is: not very impressive. Just about every figure has to be rounded up or down to make it fit the Procrustean framework.

From 392 to 800 is 408, not 400 years.
From 800 to 918 is 118, not 120 years.
From 918 to 1309 is 391, not 400 years.
From 1309 to 1377 is 68, not 70 years.
From 1377 to 1517 *is* 140 years – the first correct figure.
From 1517 to 1920 is 403, not 400 years.

---

[30] Luke 24:39.
[31] John 17:4.
[32] Acts 2:23.

Even by choosing his own list of the most significant events in European history, Moon cannot make the dates fit. The explanation, apparently, is that there are two types of numbers – 'actual' numbers, in which two and two make four, and 'prophetic' or 'symbolic' numbers, in which two and two may make five or six or thereabouts. But if numbers can mean whatever you want, their value as a proof of anything vanishes immediately.

'According to statistical understanding,' continues Sudo, 'plus or minus 2.5% error can come from meaningless random factors.'[33] But we are talking about God! Is *he* at the mercy of 'meaningless random factors'? And even if we allow him 2.5% error, his sums still fail to come out. At least one item on the list above is nearly 3% off target. What does this say about Unification numerology? And what does it suggest about Moon's messianic claims?

Apart from the numbers, often the historical parallels will not work either. Simple judgments have to be made about the life-work of extremely complex figures; detailed philosophical concepts have to be reduced to a few facile words, to force them into the scheme. *Divine Principle* does not really bring satisfaction to the sophisticated brain of modern man; rather is it an insult to his intelligence.

Will the Messiah come from Korea? Revelation 7:2 (see p.17) cannot really be called in evidence. For one thing, the preceding verse mentions four more angels, and there is nothing to give the impression that the fifth angel is somehow superior to the others. 'The rising of the sun', whatever it meant in Jewish apocalyptic, would not have meant the Orient countries; and why consider only China, Japan and Korea? What of Vietnam, Indonesia, Taiwan?

The other passage pressed into service is Matthew 21:43 (see p. 17) (though if Matthew is as 'slanted' as Moon teaches, perhaps it is unsafe to build a crucial doctrine on this passage!) But all that this parable says is that God's purposes will be taken away from the Jews and given to

[33] *120 Day Training Program*, p. 293.

another people. For two millennia Christians have applied this promise to the church, 'the Israel of God'[34] as Paul put it, and this reading makes excellent sense alongside the many New Testament passages which speak of God's promises as passing from Israel to the church. What does not make sense is to begin to reinterpret the text, on the basis of no biblical evidence whatsoever, so as to narrow down God's chosen people to one tiny nation again.

Did Jesus say he would come back in person, or with another identity? If it were true that all the Jews expected Elijah to come back in person, then there might be a case for believing that Moon is Jesus. But most of the Jews had no such expectations; and the passage in Malachi which promises Elijah's coming is an exceedingly metaphorical one. It talks about the tents of Jacob, when the tribes were no longer living under canvas. It speaks of evildoers being burned up like stubble, although nobody imagined this would literally happen. 'Elijah' is obviously a metaphorical description of the coming of someone else, *like* Elijah.

By contrast, there is nothing metaphorical or poetic about the clear New Testament promises of Jesus that he would come again, personally, unmistakably.

> I will see you again and your hearts will rejoice, and no-one will take your joy from you.[35]

The point was reinforced by the angels who appeared to the disciples immediately after Jesus' ascent into heaven:

> This Jesus, who was taken up from you into heaven, will come in the same way as you saw him go into heaven.[36]

There is only one Lord of the Second Advent envisaged in

---
[34] Galatians 6:16.
[35] John 16:22.
[36] Acts 1:11.

the New Testament, and that is Jesus. Until Sun Myung Moon can arrange to descend from the clouds in heavenly glory, his claims look singularly unimpressive.

Conclusion

'It cannot be considered as a Christian church.' This was the conclusion of the USA's National Council of the Churches of Christ, after an exhaustive study of Unification thought.[37] 'We consider it a pseudo-religion,' reported Kim Kwan Suk of the Korean National Council of Churches.[38] Christian churches all over the world have rejected Unification's claim to Christian recognition.

This conclusion is inescapably correct. Moon himself has stated, 'God is now throwing Christianity away and establishing a new religion, and this new religion is Unification Church.'[39] 'The Christians are the ones who hate us most,' he asserts; 'they hate us because Satan is in them.'[40] To Moon's mind, Christians rank pretty low; their religion could even turn out to have been Satanic:

> But still Christianity isn't the kingdom of God. Christianity is just the midway position. It must be decided whether Christianity belongs to God or Satan.[41]

Christians have no advantages over Hindus or Buddhists in the spiritual world. 'They don't do anything especially evil and they don't do any special goodness:

---

[37] *The Tablet* (2 July, 1977); *cf.* 'A Critique of the Theology of the Unification Church as Set Forth in *Divine Principle*', National Council of the Churches of Christ Commission on Faith and Order (New York, 1977), p. 10.

[38] *Yearbook* of the National Council of Churches of Korea (1972), pp. 57–58.

[39] *Time*, 30 Sept. 1974.

[40] Quoted in speech by Paul Rose MP, House of Commons, 23 Feb. 1977 (HMSO).

[41] *120 Day Training Program*, p. 109.

midway position.'[42] Many Christians think that they are going to heaven, he says, but in fact are destined for hell.

Yet, despite his private disdain, Moon goes on claiming to be a prophet of the Christian God. How can this be possible? His revelations disagree completely with previous revelation about the nature of God: and prophets who try to propagate a distorted view of God are condemned out of hand in Deutoronomy 13:1–3. He is often wrong (1967, for example, was not the start of an age of perfection); and Deuteronomy 18 warns against the prophet whose words fail to come true.

But then, according to many observers of the movement, the Unification Church has a flexible approach to truth and falsehood. There is disturbing evidence – as we shall see next – that honesty is not always Unification policy.

5
Beneath the surface

'You're sure you're nothing to do with the Unification Church?' I queried.

'Nothing at all,' he replied. 'Well, we have a few things in common, I suppose. It's like a different denomination, like Methodists and Baptists.'

I didn't believe him. The name on his leaflet, 'Federation for World Peace and Unification', sounded suspicious. But I decided to go to his meeting anyway. And there I found out the truth: I had been speaking to the head of the local Unification Church community.

I had just been subjected to an example of 'heavenly

[42] *Ibid.*, p. 225.

deception' – a favourite tactic, say many observers, in street witnessing. Since the world is in the grip of Satan, they believe it makes sense for them to fight Satan with Satan's methods. Lying and deceiving are permissible – *if* it is done for the greater glory of Father.

'In my thirteen years of observation,' remarked Robert Roland, 'this tactic of "heavenly deceit" underlies the entire movement, from the top echelon to the lowest.'[1] For a professedly Christian organization, the Unification Church has been accused of a staggering amount of duplicity. In 1977, for example, the Moon 'front' organization known as the Korean Cultural and Freedom Foundation had its fund-raising licence revoked in New York State. According to the State Social Welfare Board, it had raised £750,000 for 'child relief' – and used *less than 7%* of it for that purpose.

The Unification Church uses as many 'aliases' as some second hand car dealers, ranging from 'One World Crusade' (the most 'Christian' of its identities, designed to attract church members) to 'The Unified Family' and even 'The Kensington Gardens Arts Society' (see p. 61). The many guises make it difficult to determine the exact scope of Moon's activities and influence. In Washington, a Federal Government subcommittee report has accused Moon of organizing a group of followers to supply £600,000 from Unification Church funds so that he could unobtrusively buy control of the Diplomat National Bank. Conveniently Moon disappeared from America before the committee could subpoena him to explain the transaction.

Numbers seem to mean little to Father. In Korea he claims to have 360,000 disciples – a long way from the independently surveyed figure of 10,000 – and he has registered 935 churches in official Government reports, although an internal magazine of the Church admits that

---

[1] *Hearings before the Subcommittee on International Organisations of the Committee on International Relations, House of Representatives, Part II* (Washington, 1976), p. 15.

there are only 172.[2] Some of his disciples are equally hazy about dates; in 1977 the US Government undertook deportation proceedings against 178 Japanese Moonies who had entered the USA as temporary visitors some years before, and had 'forgotten' – or so it seemed – to go home.

There is something deceptive, too, in the image which the Church projects to outsiders. The effusive expression of affection which has drawn many lonely people into the cult soon shows through as a superficial, pragmatic veneer. The Unification Church's 'love' for people can disappear with amazing rapidity as soon as the potential convert becomes a problem. This is what happened to a boy called Tony, whose father claims he was simply dumped.

> On the afternoon of 31st January I had a phone call to say Tony was on his way home and would be arriving about 8 pm. Well, he was brought in, he didn't recognise anybody, didn't speak, just a vacant expression on his face. The two ladies made a quick exit saying they had a train to catch back to London (I later realised they had come by car). It wasn't till they had gone that I realised what Tony was really like. He wouldn't, or couldn't, eat or drink, so we got him straight to bed. We even had to undress him and put him into bed. He was also incontinent. I called the doctor the next morning, he came and said he would have to go into hospital...[3]

The Church can be very awkward to outsiders who dare to question its ways. A Christian youth organization near my home, which had risked printing an information leaflet on the church, found that someone had retaliated by printing hundreds of offensive postcards and mailing them

[2] *The Times*, 3 April 1978.
[3] Paul Rose, speech, p. 2.

to the youth organization's 'Freepost' address. The postmarks, from all over Britain, were of towns where there was a Unification centre. Each card cost the youth group 8p to receive.

It is not wise to have an illegitimate baby in the Unification Church. There will be precious little sympathy, and no practical help. The erring member may simply be turned out on the street.

> 'I have baby.' Can you stay in Unification Church? Can you ask money from Church Director to take care of the new born baby properly? Can you explain the situation to the Centre Director? No. Then they both must disappear.[4]

But deception and lovelessness are only two of the Unification Church's less appealing traits. The deeper one peers into the murk of Unification practices, the more disturbing are the facts one uncovers. The rest of this chapter will discuss just three more unsettling implications.

The spirit connection

Many people who have managed to meet Sun Myung Moon have testified to his personal charisma. 'When he walked into the room,' Shelley Liebert recalled, 'you felt blown against the wall.'[5] The magnetism of Moon's personality explains how the Church manages to believe, and circulate, stories about the expensive limousine which came running up to Father at 200 miles an hour, swearing to kill him if he wouldn't accept it; about the time Father visited the zoo, and all the animals came running over to where he stood; about the mysterious spiritual vibrations which surround his person.

From the earliest days, Father has been a priceless

[4] *120 Day Training Program*, p. 129.
[5] Enroth, *Youth, Brainwashing and the Extremist Cults*, p. 108.

spiritual asset for the Church to protect. Even back at the beginning, when Moon went on to a street-car in Korea, several members of the Church would stand in a close circle around him to protect him from the 'low spiritual vibrations' of other passengers. Toilets had to be completely cleansed and renewed before he could use them; and at Church mansions today, inordinate sums can be spent on replacing every item of culinary equipment before Moon arrives on a visit. Everything he eats must be washed with great care and in a prayerful attitude; elaborate instructions exist about the preparation of food, the colour schemes which are acceptable, even the way in which bowls of fruit must be arranged.

These fastidious arrangements are not simply a mark of respect to the Messiah, however. They reflect the Unification Church belief that there are evil spirits everywhere, and that unless they are carefully warded off they will wreak havoc in any unsuspecting person's life. Superstitions abound in Church circles. Dust is sometimes held to be a natural home for evil spirits, and members will sweep obsessively around and under their beds in case there should be a few particles of dangerous dust lying around. Some disciples have taken to carrying bags of salt around with them, sleeping with the bedroom light on, or sleeping with an open copy of *Divine Principle* placed upon their hearts. 'Holy Salt' must be sprinkled on everything – rooms, houses, food, clothing, cars, bicycles – in order to 'separate' these things from Satan and reclaim them for God. If there is no Holy Salt left to sanctify your meal with, some followers have been taught, you must blow on the food three times. And they must remember that some evil spirits are very stupid; when 'sanctifying' a room, it is vital to open the doors and windows first – otherwise the less intelligent evil spirits may not be able to find their own way out.

In view of its importance, it is fortunate that 'multiplying' Holy Salt is quite a simple matter. One merely has to buy some ordinary salt from the shops (although for some reason it mustn't be iodized); then divide it into seven roughly equal piles, pray over it in the joint names of Father, Son, Holy Spirit, True Parents and oneself; and finally sprinkle the remaining grains of one's previous Holy Salt supply on each pile.

One of the things which can be done with Holy Salt is the staking out of Holy Ground. A particular plot of land can be reclaimed from Satan, and consecrated to the powers of goodness, by sprinkling it with the Salt; it will then become an inspirational place to pray in, and a power source for witness, for as long as required. To make it a permanent Holy Ground, however, earth (called 'Holy Soil') and even a Holy Pebble have to be imported from the original Holy Ground in Korea. When they are buried a prescribed number of feet under the ground, the Holiness becomes perpetual.

Trees can be blessed, as well (the Stanton Fitzwarren commune in England calls itself the 'Holy Oak Community'); and apparently quite a familiar sight for early-morning joggers in Hyde Park is a procession of Moonies from Lancaster Gate, who visit the tree blessed by Moon there for a time of prayer each morning.

Spirits are everywhere, influencing all that happens. 'Everything is somebody's move in the cosmic battle.'[6] Lofland records that the early Moonies in America used to scan the newspapers for evidence of Satan's activity against them. When high winds and floods killed 300 people in Germany in February 1962, Satan was exacting retribution under the 'law of indemnity' for a conversion which had taken place in America that month. There were no crises in April, because God had mercifully restrained Satan in view of the arranged Unification Parents' Day. In May, Satan's efforts redoubled, and the stock market dropped.

This paranoid, fascination with the powers of evil is a

[6] J. Lofland, *Doomsday Cult* (New York, revised edn., 1977), p. 197.

long way from the Bible's perspective on Satan. True, in the Bible the devil is presented as a real, dangerous and powerful enemy; but he is a defeated enemy, with no power to invade the life or influence the circumstances of any real Christian. 'Resist the devil', advises James, 'and he will flee from you.'[7] No need for Holy Salt or a retreat to 'reclaimed' ground; the power of prayer will do.

Ironically, it is possible that the Unification Church has a lot more to do with evil spirits than its members realize. As we have noticed, a great deal of emphasis is placed upon the authority of spirit visions and manifestations. The spirit experiences which members of the Church claim to have had are among their strongest reasons for believing that Moon is the Messiah. One Moonie couldn't understand how the Bible and *Divine Principle* fitted together – they seemed incompatible – but a convenient vision cleared up the problem:

> I was very tired and thought I would rest my eyes for a while. I had only laid down when someone appeared to me in spirit. He was saying in a crying, begging voice: 'My Epistle must be rewritten.' This was said over and over again. I said: 'Who are you?' and he said: 'I am the Apostle Paul.' He seemed to be in such a state of suffering.[8]

Korea must be the chosen land, says *Divine Principle*, because spiritual signs regarding the Lord of the Second Advent's coming there 'are appearing like mushrooms after a rain'.

Therefore, countless men of religion are receiving very clear revelations . . . by contacting many spirit men of various levels . . . Nevertheless, the leaders of the present Christian world, due to their spiritual ignor-

[7] James 4:7.
[8] Lofland, *Doomsday Cult*, p. 224.

ance, are still unresponsive, and have refused to pay heed to such things.[9]

But perhaps 'spiritual ignorance' is more attributable to Father Moon and his followers than to the Christian leaders. The Christians at least know that the Bible consistently warns against any trafficking with evil spirits; that it speaks of the likelihood of contacting lying, deceiving spirits sent by the 'father of lies'[10]; that it is pointless to endeavour to contact dead men when there is a living God prepared to reveal himself to us.[11] The Unification Church has absolutely no safeguard against deception by impostor spirit powers; it naïvely trusts in anything the spirit world tells it to believe (except, of course – as we've seen earlier – when the evil spirit contradicts Moon). The potential for exploitation by evil powers is tremendous, and in Moon literature one sees hints occasionally that their entanglement with the occult isn't all straightforward and happy.

> If you leave the person [a possessed person who has been exorcised] another evil spirit may come or the same one may come back . . . In case it's impossible to stop the possession, sometimes you must send the person to a hospital.[12]

Many people within the Unification Church have become 'possessed', and it has led to some bizarre suicides (including the young man who wandered from Barrytown to the nearby railway line, and lay naked on the tracks to be decapitated by a train). Much of this may be explained by mental disturbance, arising from the thought-control techniques we shall examine later; but there is at least the

[9] *Divine Principle*, p. 529.
[10] Jude 6; Matthew 25:41; Luke 10:17; 2 Corinthians 11:14–15; Eph 6:12.
[11] Isaiah 8:19.
[12] *120 Day Training Program*, p. 146.

dark, ominous possibility that a movement which has been dabbling in the spirit world since 1936 may be introducing its unsuspecting followers to the power of demonic, destructive enemies.

Money-making

One of Jesus' parables concerns a man who arranged a great feast and then found himself without guests. The answer, he found, was to send his servants out into the highways and byways to bring in the poor, the maimed, the lame and the blind. They came readily.

Ever since Jesus first told the story, the Christian church has had a special interest in the poor and the disadvantaged. Two thousand years of medical, social and missionary enterprise bear witness to the emphasis of Jesus' ideas. But the Lord of the Second Advent has slightly different priorities: 'Father said we should always look for a millionaire,' Elizabeth Bateson instructed other Moonies, 'or we should look for a leader.'[13]

Looking for millionaires has paid off. In New York alone, Moon has been able to acquire properties ranging from the Fifth Avenue Tiffany building (£1.2 million), the 2,000-room New Yorker Hotel (£2.5 million) and the 76 Manhattan Centre (£500,000), to the Columbia University Club (£600,000) and a Long Island confectionery factory (£350,000). He also owns over 760 acres of land and property in the area – 350 in Barrytown, 410 in Westchester.

Of course, not all of the money comes from wealthy admirers. Moon has boasted, a little incautiously perhaps, of just how much his street fund-raisers can raise:

> When I mobilize 10,000 members it means thirty million dollars a month. Then we can buy Pan American Airlines and the Empire State Building. We shall buy the Ford Motor Company.[14]

[13] *Ibid.*, p. 360.
[14] *The Times*, 5 April 1978.

Great pressure is placed on converts to make money for Father. In 1973 British disciples were urged to

> get on with selling . . . Sell fast. Go like the blazes!!! – Be adventurous for God. He will protect you and yours. He will be right behind you. Remember, when you are out on the pavement doing your bit for Father, that you are the children of True Parents. Think of the leader. Think of him wearing a crown as the King of Kings.[15]

The *Training Program* urges missionaries to 'make green bills [*i.e.* dollars] happy' by winning them for Moon. 'They are all destined to go to Father . . . Messiah must be the richest . . . unless the Messiah can have dominion over things neither God nor the Messiah can be happy.'[16] And the strangest things can be done to make Messiah happy. Moonies in Southern California were instructed that, if they ran out of candy to sell, they should buy proprietary brands from a store and re-sell it for a profit. Shelley Liebert recalls, 'It didn't matter what you sold. Sometimes we didn't even take the price tag off. It was marked thirty-nine cents, and we would sell it for two dollars. We would buy products from a grocery store and re-sell them in their own parking lot.'[17]

But the Church's own products can also be immensely profitable. Candles can be sold at anything up to a 500% profit. In 1972, 400 Japanese church members entered the USA on tourist and visitor visas, and worked from dawn to dusk selling candles from door to door. Their reported profits were between $10,000 and $15,000 per day.

'How about dollar bills in your pocket?' continues the *Training Program*. 'Happy or not?' If members received money from their 'physical' parents, they were not to keep it for themselves. 'This is not making the money happy.

---

[15] *The Family News*, Feb. 1973.
[16] *120 Day Training Program*, p. 72.
[17] Enroth, *Youth, Brainwashing and the Extremist Cults*, p. 115.

We must donate or offer it. This is the principle of the Unification Church. Because of this point we may lose eternal life...'[18]

Moon has always been keen, it seems, to extract as much money as possible from the faithful. There is an amazing story in the *Training Program* about the early days in Korea, when Moon is reputed to have gathered his poverty-stricken, 'starving' membership and directed them to give him all the money they had. With it, he bought expensive clothes and instruments to begin a girls' dancing team. Not surprisingly, 'people got angry with Father ... He has no right. He is cruel. They must have felt this way. But Father didn't.'[19]

After ten years, however, the dancing team came to America, and were so successful that Father Moon was able to negotiate the one thing that made it all worthwhile – an audience with President Eisenhower. The *Training Program* implies that this demonstrates Father's far-seeing wisdom. One wonders if his starving Korean followers were equally impressed.

Nowadays, claim ex-members, similar exploitation goes on; volunteers work from 6.30 am until after midnight if necessary, and because of their status as 'volunteers' they forfeit their state pension rights. They do not pay national insurance contributions, and Moon has no intention of doing so on their behalf.

But to be fair to Moon, he makes no attempt to conceal his intentions. If not to the general public, at least to his followers, he has spelt out the cost of following Messiah:

> Even in the Communistic army they are financially supported. They are given food, clothing, arms – but I am going to use you, trying to get money out of you. Are

[18] *120 Day Training Program*, p. 73.
[19] *Ibid.*, pp. 255–256.

you ready to follow that kind of a leader? You must be crazy people.[20]

Well, he said it.

Political ambitions

Moon's theological ideas may be weird, but if he were simply another sub-Christian cult leader – the latest figure in a long line which includes Charles Taze Russell, Herbert Armstrong and Joseph Smith – few people apart from believing Christians would be at all concerned about him. As it is, there are several questionable non-religious aspects to his operations which keep him at the centre of international controversy.

One of his own church's documents admits that Moon is only a church leader by accident – because that seemed the best way of influencing people.

> Since a church is the safest and most recognized form of social organization, Mr Moon founded the church in 1954 in order to have the greatest freedom of action.[21]

'Are you aware,' Allen Tate Wood asked American Congressmen, 'that your constituents are being defrauded into sponsoring the dreams of a man who tells his mesmerised followers that God is about to phase out democracy?

'Did you know that Mr Moon, on occasion, has told his followers that it would be better for them to commit suicide than fail in their responsibility to him?

'Did you know that Mr Moon has told his followers that if he fails, they should march into the sea?'[22]

---

[20] Quoted in Enroth, *Youth, Brainwashing and the Extremist Cults*, p. 111.
[21] Quoted in *Hearings*, p. 36.
[22] Allen Tate Wood, in *Hearings*, p. 21.

Moon's political ambitions are truly staggering. He has instructed his church that the United Nations 'must be annihilated by our power,'[23] that existing Senators and Congressmen may be replaced by new ones drawn from his own followers, that 'the whole world is in my hands and I will conquer and subjugate the world'.[24] His words, he says, will serve as law, and whatever he says will immediately be done.[25]

The key to his political ambitions is his hatred of Communism. Until 1974, one of his manifold enterprises in Korea was the Kuri Anti-Communist Training Centre, where with government support he ran courses on the threat of Marxism for village chiefs, army reserves and officials. An anti-Marxist theme runs through *Divine Principle* from beginning to end. For the *Training Program*, the greatest of enemies – the focus of Satan's love and affection – is North Korean Communist chief Kim Il Sung:

> If Communism comes to have dominion over the world, it won't be Russia or Red China, but Kim Il Sung who will have dominion over the world.[26]

The Unification assessment of historical figures is determined by the effect they had upon Korea. The end of the Korean War in 1953, merciful though it may have seemed, was President Truman's great failure; 'it was Satanic'. The Vietnam War was inspired by God; 'only a Satanic movement approves being against this war'. And Richard Nixon, Watergate notwithstanding, was the 'best president throughout the history of America' because of one act: he visited China in 1972, thus (theoretically) pre-

[23] Barry Morrison, 'The Unification Church: The Struggle of a New Religious Movement' (London, 1978), p. 5.
[24] *Ibid.*, p. 4.
[25] Rose, speech, p. 4.
[26] *120 Day Training Program*, p. 98.

venting Kim Il Sung from declaring war on the south. This made Nixon 'the first President of America who fulfilled his mission'. Should anyone object that Nixon fulfilled lots of other things, too, some of them a trifle dubious, the *Training Program* counters that the USA lost Nixon as President because of its 'disobedience to God's will'[27] – not because of Nixon's disobedience to the US Constitution.

Because of Moon's political views, there have been many attempts to trace a link between the Church and the repressive South Korean government. It seems indubitable that some link must exist. Said Donald Ranard, former head of the US State Department Korean desk:

> No organization of this size with a Korean base could exist without some linkage to the Korean government. When the KCIA has infiltrated Christian churches in Korea to the extent it has, isn't it peculiar that an offbeat Korean church is moving ahead so rapidly and gaining members without help from the Korean Government?[28]

It is significant that the Unification Church appears to be the only group which has not suffered from the late Korean dictator's edicts suppressing civil liberties. John Lofland points out that despite an edict banning mass rallies, in 1975 Moon was able to stage a pro-government rally which 1,200,000 people are reported to have attended. 'This is the equivalent', remarked former Moon aide Allen Tate Wood, 'of John the Baptist holding a pro-government demonstration in Jerusalem in support of King Herod.'[29]

Needless to say, the Church denies any political link with the Korean dictatorship. But Lee Jai Hyon (now a

[27] *Ibid.*, pp. 103–106.
[28] *The Times*, 3 April 1978.
[29] Rose, speech, p. 4.

professor at Western Illinois University, but formerly a Korean government official for twenty years) has testified that Moon's associate Colonel Pak Bo Hi used to have access to the Korean Embassy's cable channel to the highest levels of South Korean government. Colonel Pak at one time combined the job of Moon's American representative with that of assistant military attaché at the embassy, and Robert Roland – a close associate at that time – remembers how closely intertwined the two activities were.

> He further told me directly and implied numerous times that their movement was looked upon with favour by the South Korean Government . . . A military attaché was giving him a difficult time for neglecting his embassy duties because of his Moon efforts . . . but this colonel was the only one in the embassy who resisted his efforts on behalf of Moon, and this stemmed from the colonel's personal dislike for Pak. Pak continued by saying he would get Moon's work done if it meant working 24 hours a day.
> Pak indicated that his primary aim was to establish influential contacts with the governmental and social elite of the Nation's Capital.[30]

Pak has of course issued blanket denials, in a document entitled *A Historic Defence*, which contains a host of allegations but remarkably few specific facts. The testimony of Roland and Lee, however, seems to fit in with Moon's private ambitions, as revealed in his secret speeches.

> Unless we are powerful, we cannot save this Nation [the USA]. Perhaps in 3 years Senators will come to take our State Representatives to their place in luxurious cars, and they will put themselves at his disposal.

[30] *Hearings*, p. 15.

That is what is happening in Korea.[31]

> Master will assign three young ladies to each Senator ... To restore the Senators you must make the aides your friends, particularly secretaries.
>
> Master needs many good-looking girls – 300 ... If our girls are superior to the Senators in many ways, then the Senators will just be taken by our members.[32]

While Shelley Liebert was housekeeper of Moon's mansion in Pasadena, one of her jobs was to cook and clean for the 'public relations girls'. These privileged Moonies had a large expense account and several unusual privileges; they would get up late and work for only a few hours each day. 'I didn't get to be one', recalls Shelley, 'because I guess I didn't fit the image ... I just didn't have the glow of health that was required.'[33]

The Church's public-relations exercises in US government circles are conducted with a view to their effect upon Moon's prestige in Korea. Neil Salonen, Moon's American chief, made this clear in an internal document for church members.

> When Father came to the United States his primary purpose was to do things to make him influential in Korea.
>
> The Day of Hope Tour and specially the rallies in support of President Nixon were far more significant due to the impact they had in Korea than their impact here ... If it was important in Korea and if it helped to bring the Government and our church close together then it was more important than anything else.[34]

---

[31] *Ibid.*, p. 19.
[32] Lofland, *Doomsday Cult*, p. 297 (quotations date from Dec. 1971 and May 1973 respectively).
[33] Enroth, *Youth, Brainwashing and the Extremist Cults*, p. 105.
[34] *The Times*, 4 April 1978.

More important than anything else – because Korea is the land of destiny, 'God's chosen nation'. Lofland found that in 'safe company' Moonies would refer to Korea as 'the motherland' and revealed 'strong beliefs in . . . Koreans as a superpeople'.[35] Despite all the compliments he has paid to Britain and the USA Moon has never deigned to learn English. Why should he? Korea is destined to lead the world!

Some ex-members of the cult, who had spent over two years in Moon circles, have spoken of their signing a pledge to fight for Korea in the event of a war. Pak is reported to have stated, 'I can envision Divine Principle Soldiers crossing the 38th parallel fully armed.'[36] And at a conference in Seoul in June 1975, the Church passed a resolution to establish an international corps of volunteers, prepared in case of war to 'defend South Korea to the death.'[37] In Unification thought, religion and politics come very close together.

What sort of a world does Moon want to establish? Not surprisingly, in view of his tacit approval of the late President Park, it won't be a democratic one. Democracy was all very well, but 'monarchism' achieves results faster.

> Just imagine if America is monarchic and the President of America is like a king. If only he can understand *Divine Principle,* and if he can receive the Messiah and bow to him, then he has the absolute authority to cover all of the American people.[38]

So much for civil rights. Ken Sudo goes on to fantasize about entire nations being compelled to watch obligatory TV programmes which will instruct them in *Divine Principle*. If it's good for them, never mind whether or

[35] Lofland, *Doomsday Cult*, p. 26.
[36] *Hearings*, p. 16.
[37] Robert Key, 'Followers of Mr Moon' (Oxford, 1978).
[38] *120 Day Training Program*, p. 295.

not they *want* to be converted.

How would Moon's world monarchy operate? The basic unit, says Lofland, would be the New Age family, headed by a father and mother who had been re-matched and re-married by Moon. Families would live in groups of three, and each group of three would be under the authority of another group of three, all the way up the pyramid to the very top family of all – needless to say, the family of Sun Myung Moon. This very tight, authoritarian structure would be vital because evil thoughts might still be about at the bottom of the heap. 'Other proximate families would be able to "spiritually detect" deviationist tendencies and bring quick corrective action.'[39] One begins to wonder whether Moon has ever read *Nineteen Eighty-four*.

It sounds sinister, but also most improbable; and as a serious political threat Moon can probably be discounted. Yet it makes it all the more incredible that the Unification Church is able to influence intelligent young people – many of them students who previously had left-wing tendencies – and sell them such an amazing package of political wishful thinking. What is the secret of the Church's success? Honest persuasion – or the 'brainwashing', 'mind manipulation' and 'indoctrination' alleged by the sensational press?

6
'I am your brain'

Rosalind Mitchell's parents are in the Unification Church. 'They're just not the same people', she says. 'It's like meeting strangers who are wearing my parents' skins.'[1]

[39] Lofland, *Doomsday Cult*, p. 27.
[1] *Titbits* (18–24 Nov. 1976), p. 6.

Tony Adamson's mother feels similarly about her son. 'He is a polite stranger I can no longer recognise ... After A-levels, the very next day he joined the UC. He did not even wait to find out the results of his exams.'[2]

What does the Unification Church do to its members? Are the fears of parents groundless flights of fancy? Or is the atmosphere of the Church as one mother described it – 'what hell would truly be like; a world of mindless automatons under one absolute controlling force'?[3]

The Church hotly resents the use of the word 'brainwashing' to describe its activities. Experts are not so sure. Dr Margaret Singer, a lecturer in psychology at the University of California, compares Moon training techniques with the brainwashing methods used on American prisoners of war in Korea. Dr Ernest Giovanoli of New York, a psychiatrist who has had to piece together the shattered lives of Barrytown 'failures', openly uses the word 'brainwashing' about what his patients have experienced. And Dr John Clark, Assistant Clinical Professor at Harvard Medical School, concludes a paper on the subject with these words:

> Their conversion and indoctrination processes result in changes which are regressive both to the society and the long-term health of their victims. Their methods must be studied before another series of major political catastrophes becomes inevitable.[4]

Paul Engel joined the Church after meeting a missionary in California. He was assured that New Education Development – the 'front' name used by the missionary – was not connected with Sun Myung Moon, and accepted

[2] Diana Patt, 'Growing Protests about Moon Cult Activities' (Bromley, 1978), p. 1.

[3] Paul Engel, 'The World of the Cult' (New York, 1977), p. 7.

[4] J. G. Clark, 'The Manipulation of Madness', paper presented in Hanover, West Germany, Feb. 1978.

the invitation to dinner that evening. At dinner he found himself the centre of attention, fussed over and praised by an energetic, clean-cut group of people.

They persuaded him to attend a weekend seminar, and this he found tougher going. 'The activity was so intense and incessant, I had no time to think about it. The only time I had for myself was during sleep. Every minute was accounted for.'[5] But all the same, the feeling of being loved and valued by virtual strangers was so unusual and gratifying that he was easily persuaded into a week-long seminar on their North Californian farm.

Here, he found, he was completely cut off from the outside world. A newspaper which he contrived to obtain was gently confiscated from his belongings. With no radio or TV, all the conversations ranged around *Divine Principle*. The lectures became progressively more emotional, and if through tiredness anyone dozed off, he would be made to stand or have his back rubbed. Gradually, through fatigue, emotional battering and constant repetition of Moon theology, it became very difficult to think independently.

Pressure was placed on him to remain for another week. And another. In the most emotive lecture of all, at the end of the first week, came the clinching revelation: Sun Myung Moon was Messiah! From his previous contact with the cult, Paul had suspected that this was what the lectures were leading towards – but even so, 'I found myself getting emotionally involved in the reading, a recitation of Christ's sufferings, and the subsequent deep personal prayer.'[6]

After three weeks, Paul was sent out into the streets to sell flowers. But far from being restored to normality by this, he found that three intense weeks of indoctrination had so 'institutionalized' him that he panicked at the thought of having to live outside the cult. He was 'hooked'.

[5] Engel, 'The World of the Cult', p. 2.
[6] *Ibid.*, p. 3.

Now that they had turned him into a Church worker, his leaders cut down his sleeping hours from eight a night to four. He was given very little protein food, but plenty of unhealthy carbohydrates. In his fatigued state he did whatever the church wanted of him; if he wished to think for himself, there were only his sleeping hours to do it in.

This state of affairs could have continued indefinitely, but for an accident which forced him to think again and led to his escape. But his experience is typical of many others (although some sources claim that the Church's methods in California, under Moses Durst, are more ruthless than those employed elsewhere). And it throws some light on Father Moon's cryptic words:

> If there appears a crack in the man's personality, you wedge in a chisel, and split the person apart.[7]

One of the most readily available 'cracks' is physical fatigue, and the Church seems to have used it mercilessly. Lectures can be allowed to drag on until late at night; spare-time study will be requested by the lecturer, but no time will be allowed for it, and so students will have to use their sleep time in order to catch up. Should they fall ill, they may be told that their illness is Satanic:

> When you feel sick, don't say to yourself, 'Oh, I feel sick, therefore I must go to bed.' Don't think this way. Okay? This feeling is Satanic. When you are feverish and very sick, you must go to bed; but pray to God, 'Oh Heavenly Father, I am sorry. I must keep your body healthy . . . ' Apologize to Heavenly Father because you could not keep well.[8]

Anyone who commits a sin must work three times as hard as anyone else. And a good way of improving the power of one's prayers is to take on a 'condition' – a kind

[7] Rose, speech, p. 4.
[8] *120 Day Training Program*, p. 69.

of endurance project which can consist of prayer, fasting, or even cold showers. 'Conditions' last for a minimum of three days.

Physical desires must be kept strictly in check. Sex is not exactly evil, but neither is it recommended:

> Married couples must abstain from the marriage relationship for at least seven months. There are those in Korea who have been abstaining for over seven years and live as sister and brother.
> Those whom God loves cannot continue their married life. God strikes at their bodies and they cannot continue.[9]

And apart from these physical devices to keep members in their place, the Church has at least four powerful psychological weapons which it can use to enforce obedience. The first is *emotionalism*. There is a lot of loud, rhythmical singing in Moon centres, much arm-linking and back-slapping. Lectures are full of dramatic gestures, theatrical changes of tone and style, and communal expressions of emotion are encouraged. Bill and Ian Hall were horrified by what they experienced in the Dunbar centre of the Church:

> We had to go into a room and bow three times in front of a massive picture of Sun Myung Moon. Then we all had to say our own sort of prayers.
> It began very quietly and then built up into a crescendo of shouting people. Then they started hissing. It was like a vipers' nest.
> It was terrifying. Like something out of *The Exorcist*.[10]

They were told that the purpose of the hissing was to drive out wrong thoughts from one's system. The connections

[9] Patt, 'Growing Protests about Moon Cult Activities', p. 3.
[10] *Swindon Evening Advertiser*, 20 Oct. 1977.

with *Nineteen Eighty-four* and the 'three-minute hate', are obvious. Communal excitement and emotion are a strong psychological safeguard against doubting, negative, original thought.

A second 'weapon' is the use of *concentrated love*. One disciple described in the *Training Program* how each newcomer to a centre had been assigned to a Church member who would stay with the novice all day long, never leaving him even to visit the bathroom. Ken Sudo immediately commented, 'What she described is the key to success in witnessing.'[11]

Should the newcomer decide to leave, all available members will subject him to a process sometimes called 'love bombing' – tearful, affectionate appeals to stay. 'But we love you so much. Why do you want to do this to us? Why should you leave when we can give you so much?'

This concentration of attention and affection can win over a newcomer even though he sees Moon theology as quite irrational. One ex-member recalled:

> I wanted to break through that badly enough that right then it almost didn't matter what they believed – if only I could really share myself with them. I think that moment may be exactly the point at which many people decide to join.[12]

If love does not work, the third weapon is *fear*. Satan is everywhere – and now that the neophyte has learned about *Divine Principle*, Satan will be very angry with him. If he ventures out into the world again, away from the safety of the Centre, perhaps he will be run over by a bus, or invaded by Satan and driven mad. Or perhaps misfortune will befall his family. The only safe course is to stay put.

Yet even if the Centre is safe territory, Satan is always

[11] *120 Day Training Program*, p. 338.
[12] Lofland, *Doomsday Cult*, p. 69.

looking for a way in; if the new member harbours critical thoughts, Satan can take him over. Satan will work through his parents, too, if they try to take him away; he must be recognized and resisted.

> The biggest Satan is you, yourself, not others. If we can subjugate the biggest Satan within ourselves, we can subjugate any Satan anywhere in the world.[13]

The fourth psychological weapon is the logic of *the theology itself*. According to Moon, the fallen nature of man has four aspects. First, fallen man cannot see things from God's viewpoint; and so Moon's follower must accept God's viewpoint, even when it makes no sense. ('I am a thinker,' Moon explains, 'I am your brain.')[14] Secondly, man's sin involved leaving his proper position in the scheme of things; and so a Moonie must remain in his assigned position without complaint or question. Thirdly, man's sin involved a reversal of dominion – failing to obey a superior. Hence this is a heinous offence in the Church, and even thinking critically of your immediate superior incurs God's displeasure. And fourthly, man's fall involved the multiplication of sin; Eve was seduced, then in her turn seduced Adam. Therefore no two people must be allowed to establish a close enough relationship with each other for them to multiply sin. If two members were spending too much time in conversation together, the others would be expected to break in and split up the relationship. Belonging to Moon's Church can be a lonely business.

'Brainwashing'? That depends on what one takes the term to mean. But it is doubtful whether, without the use of dubious techniques – whether one calls them 'thought control', 'mind manipulation' or 'mental interference', they would have made half of the disciples they have.

---

[13] *120 Day Training Program*, p. 63.
[14] Morrison, 'The Unification Church', p. 5.

7
For Christians only

So much, then, for 'the rising of the Moon'. But what can Christians do about it? Is there any way of combating the spread of this amazing organization, and enlightening those who are entangled within it?

The average Christian, when confronted by a Moon missionary on the street, is apt to make a lot of mistakes. It is vital to remember that Moon knows a lot about evangelicals – he is from a Presbyterian background – and that his followers are carefully inoculated against the standard Christian approaches. The usual technique of giving one's personal testimony, or seeking to engage in theological debate, simply will not work. This is because Moon's followers are trained to do three things whenever they meet someone on the street.

1. *To endeavour to show 'the harmony of beliefs'*. The Moonie will induce you to express your own beliefs, so that he can then show how closely his opinions coincide with yours. Whatever you say, he will find something within it with which he will agree. He will share very little information about his distinctive beliefs, but simply try to convince you that he is on your side. Hence to tell him that you are a Christian is to play into his hands. It can be far more productive to be mysterious, to keep him wondering how to 'label' you; for in this way you force him to think, to adopt critical categories and use his personal intelligence in working out where you stand. It may be the first time he has had to think for himself within weeks.

2. *To suggest the value of experience*, of personally visiting a Moon centre and undergoing a training course. Should you try to engage him in argument about his beliefs, he will not usually take up the challenge. He has been trained to divulge as little as possible on the street, because

a three-day course is necessary to explain the *Principle* adequately.

3. *To invite you to a meeting,* dinner or weekend, where you can investigate the Church in depth. In view of the pressures which will be placed upon you if you do, it would be extremely unwise to take up such an invitation.

What, then, *can* be done with a Moon missionary? Is there a way of making an impact? There is; but two facts must be remembered. First, there is probably a psychological problem as well as a spiritual problem to be dealt with, and it is most unlikely that you will be able to sort out both in a few minutes on the street corner. Moonies will be affected only by long, patient friendship-building, and the most you can hope for on the street corner is to be able to jolt their thinking a little. Second, Unification missionaries do not always tell the truth. 'Heavenly deception' allows them to slide out of possible problems and embarrassing admissions. It is always good to have chapter and verse for any claims you make about them, as they cannot then simply deny your assertions.

The best way to create an impact is to force the missionary to consider questions about himself. How long has he been with the Church? Who are his parents? How long is it since he saw them? Since the whole ethos of the cult is designed to draw the disciple's attention away from his own personality, and to fix it relentlessly upon Father Moon, the more your questions can direct his thinking back to himself and his individual situation, the better. If you speak of Moon and the Church, do so charitably; any harsh criticism will immediately identify you as Satan's instrument, and perhaps make the missionary anxious to close the interview. If you find you must say something critical of Moon and *Divine Principle,* it is always good to apologize in advance – 'I know what I'm going to say now will sound offensive to you, and believe me, I'm not trying to upset you ... '

The Moon missionary will always claim to read his

Bible and study it regularly; but judging by the lack of scriptural knowledge evidenced by many Moonies this claim can be quite empty. So it can be useful to challenge the missionary to read through a short portion of the New Testament, if he will. It's unlikely that he will oblige, but if you have a copy of (say) John's Gospel to give away, you may just spark off his interest.

On the rare occasions when it is possible to have an extended friendship with a Moonie it can make a sizeable impact to introduce him to the atmosphere of a relaxed, happy Christian home. Since so much of the Moon doctrine relates to marriage, he will be much more impressed by the spectacle of a contented, working Christian marriage than by the forceful arguments of an individual.

Finally, it is always important to remember that the encounter between a Moon follower and yourself is not merely a clash of wills, a contest of wits, but a spiritual battle for which you require 'the whole armour of God'. Approach the situation with prayer, and especially afterwards remember to include the Moon contact in your prayers. Ultimately, the cleverest questions, the most sympathetic sharing, will never break down a Moonie's wall of illusion. Only the spiritual weapons of our warfare, with divine power to destroy strongholds, can ever do that.

Additional note:

Other names used by the Unification Church in Britain

Holy Spirit Association for the Unification of World Christianity
Sun Myung Moon Foundation
International Cultural Foundation
International Federation for Victory over Communism
Federation for World Peace and Unification
Council for Unified Research and Education
Unified Family Singers
Unified Family Enterprises
New Life Singers International
Cartographer Crafts Ltd
One World Crusade
Freedom Leadership Foundation
God's Light Infantry
The Weekly Religion
Carnation Appeal
Holy Oak Community
Hearts of Oak Association
Collegiate Association for Research in Principle
Kensington Gardens Arts Society

Valuable books for further reading

James Bjornstadt, *The Moon is Not the Son* (Minneapolis, 1976).

Ronald Enroth, *Youth, Brainwashing and the Extremist Cults* (Exeter, 1978).

Zola Levitt, *The Spirit of Sun Myung Moon* (Irvine, Ca., 1975).

Pat Means, *The Mystical Maze* (San Bernardino, Ca., 1977; available from Campus Crusade, 105 London Road, Reading RG1 5BY, UK).

W. J. Peterson, *Those Curious New Cults* (New Canaan, Ct., 1975).

J. Isamu Yamamoto, *The Moon Doctrine* (Downers Grove, Ill., 1976) and *The Puppet Master* (Downers Grove, Ill., 1977).